Carving Miniature Duck Decoys

Easy-to-Use Templates and
Complete Instructions
for Making 16
Decorative Carvings

Anthony Hillman

E P B M
ECHO POINT BOOKS & MEDIA, LLC
Brattleboro, Vermont

to Jennifer Hillman

Finished carvings and paintings in this book are available
directly from the author. Send an email to :
Anthony Hillman at www.hillman1948@hotmail.com
or visit his web site at www.HillmanArt.com.

Published by Echo Point Books & Media
Brattleboro, Vermont
www.EchoPointBooks.com

Carving Miniature Duck Decoys
ISBN: 978-1-64837-065-6 (paperback)

Interior design by Ed Cencora

Cover design by Kaitlyn Whitaker

How to Carve a
Miniature Duck Decoy

The first miniature decoy was carved to decorate a mantelpiece or provide a toy for a child. Miniatures were usually made by the same men who provided full-size hunting decoys for sportsmen and, in early days, for market hunters. As the great flocks of waterfowl diminished and more restrictions were imposed on hunting, carvers found a market for the miniature decoys they made during the "off season" of their trade. I suspect that these men enjoyed making these "little ducks," geese, and swans just as I find it relaxing to produce a miniature version of one of my full-size decoys.

There are advantages to carving miniatures. A minimal amount of wood can be used to produce an extremely fine carving. And miniatures occupy little space; there always seems to be room for one more miniature duck, goose, or swan on the shelf or windowsill.

To begin, select the set of patterns for the miniature you wish to carve and either cut that page free or photocopy it. The patterns in this book are drawn to a scale of 3/8":1". If you desire, glue the pattern to heavier cardboard, recut, and varnish. The patterns for each miniature consists of a profile and a top view each of both the head and the body. (A profile of a variant head—for the female, the preening position, or the like—has also been provided for some ducks. Where no female variant head is offered, the main head, as well as the body, may be used for either male or female, except in two cases: the common pintail and the oldsquaw, both of which are labeled as "male" in their plate titles.) The profiles and the top view of the body may be used as templates.

NOTE: *The top view of the head is not a template. Do not mount it on cardboard!* This will be explained below.

The head pattern has been drawn connected to the body pattern in the main profile view to give a sense of how the head and body will look together. They are to be separated for use as templates so that the head and body can be carved on separate pieces of wood. Drill a small hole in the head template to serve as a guide for positioning the eye. With the heads and bodies left connected, the profile patterns can be used for designing carved or painted plaques, needlepoint, or any other craft projects you can think of.

With each set of patterns I have provided a top view of the head. This is meant as a visual reference only, indicating how to shape the bill. Do not use it as a template, since it incorporates the effect of foreshortening, a result of the slight forward tilt of the head, making the bill look shorter than it really is.

NOTE: The dimensions given with the patterns are actual thicknesses of the *finished* miniatures. Since these patterns are small, permitting a jigsaw or a fine-bladed band saw to be used, I recommend that, for cutting, you draw the shapes on stock that is at least ½" larger in all dimensions. This will allow safe manipulation of the wood while the blade does its work. Use extreme caution when sawing out miniatures, especially on a band saw. If you are unfamiliar with such tools, a shop that does millwork will cut out the shapes for a nominal fee.

Selecting the Wood

Basswood (linden) is by far the most popular wood for carving miniatures, with clear-grained white pine running a close second. I prefer to use basswood for the heads and pine for the bodies whenever possible. There are many mail-order suppliers of carving woods, and booths where supplies are sold may be found at most of the larger bird-carving shows.

Experiment with softwoods available in your own region, since a local source is usually much more economical and convenient. Several dollars' worth of quality wood will provide enough material for many, many miniature bird carvings.

Carving the Head

When starting a miniature decoy, it is usually more convenient to carve the head first, as the shape of the partly completed neck will allow you to position the head accurately on the body. The head will demand more time and effort than the body. Generally, what you want to achieve in your carving, especially of the head, is symmetry of form. In other words, the eyes should be opposite each other! Also, both cheeks should be equally full, and the neck and top of the head should have the same graceful curves on either side.

Let's make a mallard. Lay the template for the profile of the head on a piece of basswood or other suitable wood at least 1¼″ from top to bottom. This allows plenty of excess wood so the stock can be manipulated and sawn safely. Make sure that the grain of the wood runs *with the bill*. Position the template so the base of the neck is even with the bottom edge of the wood. Trace around the template with a pencil, and cut out the shape on a jigsaw or band saw. A drill bit of the proper size can be used to cut out the tight curve under the chin area.

After sawing out the head shape, measure exactly half the thickness of your stock. With a pencil, draw a line along the middle of the entire head block on all sawn surfaces. *Never cut this line away!* It marks the cross section of the head and should remain until you give your carving its final sanding (see Figure 2).

At this point, while the sides of the head are still flat, you may want to drill guide holes for the eyes. Use a drill press if available (see Fig. 1). If you do not want to use glass eyes, a nail set (driving punch) of the proper size may be used to make a circular depression in the wood, and the eye may be painted on.

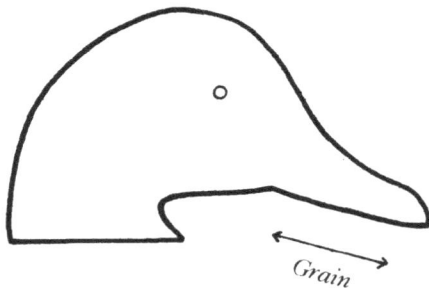

Fig. 1.
Profile of Mallard Head,
Showing Placement of Eye.

Next, with a roughing knife, taper the sides of the head from top to bottom. As you go keep checking both sides to see that they are even and symmetrical (Fig. 2).

Look at the head from the top. Make sure that the cross-section line remains clearly marked. Using the profile pattern as a guide, mark a line, perpendicular to the cross-section line, across the upper side of the bill, at its base, indicating where the top of the bill joins the head. Mark a similar line, corresponding to the line just made and also perpendicular to the cross-section line,

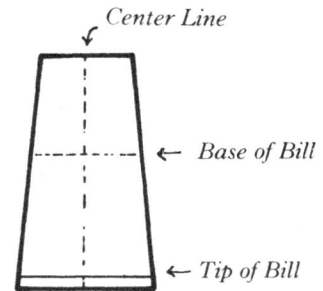

Fig. 2.
Front View of Unfinished
Mallard Head, Showing Taper.

on the underside of the bill. Generally, bill width can be approximated by marking two guidelines, one on each side of the cross-section line and parallel to it (Fig. 3). These will usually be about halfway between the center line and the outside edges of the wood. Bill widths vary depending on the species, so check the top view of the head for the particular duck you are carving.

Fig. 3.
Top View of Unfinished Mallard Head,
Showing Approximate Bill Width.

Next, carve, or saw and carve, the bill according to these guidelines, referring also to the top view and profile of the head. Make sure that the sides of the bill are symmetrical relative to the cross-section line (Fig. 4).

Fig. 4.
Front View of Partially
Finished Mallard Head.

With shovelers, a good method is to leave the forward end of the bill as wide as the head, then carve out the bill according to the top view. Whether you carve the bill first or last is a matter of personal preference. You can mark the lines for bill width and then start carving at the neck.

Carve off the corners of the neck to make it gracefully round. Carve into the eye area to help define a full cheek, and round off the top of the head (Fig. 5).

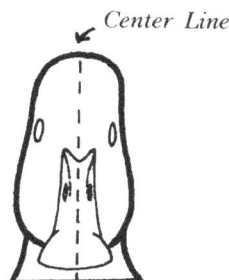

Center Line

Fig. 5.
Front View of Mallard Head.

When you are satisfied that you have done as good a carving job as your skill allows, sand the head smooth. Using the patterns and drawings as a guide, pencil in a line all around the base of the bill to mark where it meets the head (later, this will be an aid to painting). Depending on your preference, you may either carve the nostrils now or paint them on later.

If you are using glass eyes, I recommend gluing them in at this point, since doing so after the head has been glued onto the body may place too much pressure on the neck and cause it to break.

The head is now ready to be glued onto the body, which we will carve next.

Carving the Body

Place the template for the top of the body on a piece of wood at least 5¹³⁄₁₆″ long, 1⅞″ high, and 2⅝″ wide (this allows about ½″ excess wood in each dimension for cutting). Draw a line around the template and saw out the pattern. Now you are ready to use the template for the profile. Drawing the pattern directly onto the now curved sides of the wood takes some practice. One way around the difficulty is to temporarily reattach the scraps of wood you have just sawn off and trace around the template on this flat surface. You can hold the scraps in place as you carve out the profile. The main goals in carving the profile will be to remove excess wood from above and below the tail, and to create a neck shelf (the area where the head is to be fastened on) that is smooth and slopes forward at the proper angle (see the top right-hand corner of Figs. 6 and 7 for the area where the neck shelf will be created).

Before you begin carving, use a pencil to draw a guideline all around the body. This should run (on both sides) from the center of the tail to the place on the

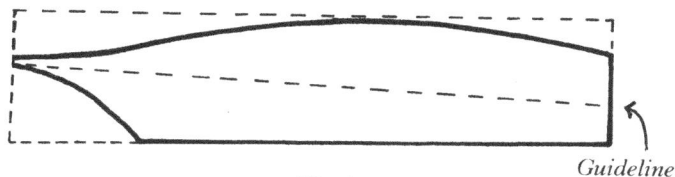

Fig. 6.
Profile of Dabbling Duck Body.

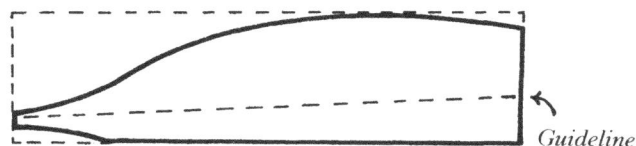

Fig. 7.
Profile of Diving Duck Body.

breast with the greatest bulge, usually about halfway down the front. As shown in Figs. 6 and 7, the greatest differences in the position of this line are between "dabbling" ducks (Plates 1–7) and "diving" ducks (Plates 8–16). Dabbling ducks float with their tails well above the water, so the guideline will slope downward from back to front; diving ducks float with their tails close to or even touching the water, so the line will be level or rise slightly from back to front. *Do not cut this guideline away!* It marks where the body of the duck bulges to its widest, and you will need it to maintain the shape indicated by the top-view pattern. It should remain until you give your miniature its final sanding.

Next you should define the neck shelf. Referring to the patterns, place the completed head where the neck shelf will be and draw a line around the base of the neck with a pencil. Note that the head does not have to point straight forward. Turning it slightly to one side will create a subtle feeling of motion.

You are now ready to carve the body. You can begin by cutting away large areas of excess wood with a fairly large knife, then switch to a smaller knife. Use the patterns and drawings and the photographs on the covers to determine the exact shapes you need to carve. Be sure to shape both sides the same way, cutting an equal amount alternately from each side.

You may wish to place the head in position from time to time as you carve areas around the base of the neck. Be careful, of course, not to cut into the penciled line you have drawn there. As you carve the tail, see that it merges gracefully with the rest of the body. Also, be sure not to carve the tail too thin, as it could easily be damaged later.

When you are satisfied that you have finished carving the body, sand it smooth with #80 sandpaper. Glue the head in place. Be sure that the glue has hardened; then sand around the line where the neck and body meet so that the neck and breast flow into each other with a smooth, continuous gradation. Using #120 sandpaper, sand once more to a smooth finish. Your miniature decoy is now completely carved and ready for finishing.

Painting or Finishing Your Miniature

There are many ways to finish your carving. Most likely you will want to either leave the natural grain of the wood visible or paint. If you wish to give the decoy a natural finish to bring out the beauty of the grain, proceed as follows. Make sure that all blemishes have been sanded out. Create an extremely smooth surface by going over the wood once again with #220 sandpaper. If you desire, stain the wood a different color, and allow to dry thoroughly. Finally, apply a coat of varnish or shellac, following the directions on the can.

If you want to paint your decoy, I can offer some basic tips and procedures here. First, study the color scheme of the species of duck represented by your miniature. The more you research your subject, the more rewarding will be the final result of your efforts, so you may want to supplement the color photographs on the covers of this book with other sources. If you can observe living birds, so much the better. In fact, this can become a most enjoyable part of your decoy-painting activities. Study skins, sharp color photographs, and accurate paintings are all helpful. Useful guides to duck coloration may be found in the bird-identification manuals of the Peterson Field Guide Series (Boston: Houghton Mifflin). My own book, *Painting Duck Decoys* (New York: Dover [24810-0], 1985), features 24 full-color plates with profiles and top views of males and females of 13 well-known species of ducks; it also includes a complete guide to painting decoys, with much more information than I have space to give here. Another excellent book with detailed information on techniques for painting bird carvings is *Game Bird Carving* (2nd ed.) by Bruce Burk (Piscataway, N.J.: Winchester Press, 1982).

Except for the common pintail and the oldsquaw, marked in the plate titles as "Male," all of the miniatures for which there are patterns in this book can be painted as either males or females. If no separate pattern for a female head appears, the single head given, along with the body—always remembering the two exceptions—is good for both. (If you use as a guide the little drawings of ducks that I have added to the plates, you should be aware that these all portray males, except for the flock of male and female common eiders on Plate 12.)

Before applying colors, you should seal and prime the wood. Sealer and primer may be purchased in any paint store. I particularly recommend "Kilz" primer-sealer, an excellent product of Masterchem Industries. This saves you a step by priming and sealing in one operation; best of all, "Kilz" can be covered with either oils or acrylics. (When using acrylics, however, it is a good idea to top the "Kilz" with a coat of an acrylic primer to insure maximum adhesion of the final coat of paint.) Primers are usually white, but they can be tinted if you desire.

After applying primer, let dry the required time, and then sand with #220 sandpaper to provide a smooth surface for painting. The question of whether to use oil or acrylic paint must be faced. Acrylics are more popular and are recommended for the beginner because they dry quickly and allow brushes to be cleaned with soap and water.

Apply paint first to large areas, using flat, solid colors first. Let dry and then apply details with a thin brush. With practice you can learn stipple and dry-brush techniques, most effective for achieving soft shading and the illusion of vermiculations. To make colors blend into each other with no discernible edge, wet-on-wet technique is in order.

There are as many different ways to paint decoys as there are decoy painters, so feel free to experiment. Eventually you will develop your own individual style, which can be as broadly stylized or as realistically detailed as you wish.

TAKING OFF

Mallard

Dimensions:
Head: 2¼" long × 1¼" high × ¾" wide
Body: 5⁵⁄₁₆" long × 1⅜" high × 2⅛" wide

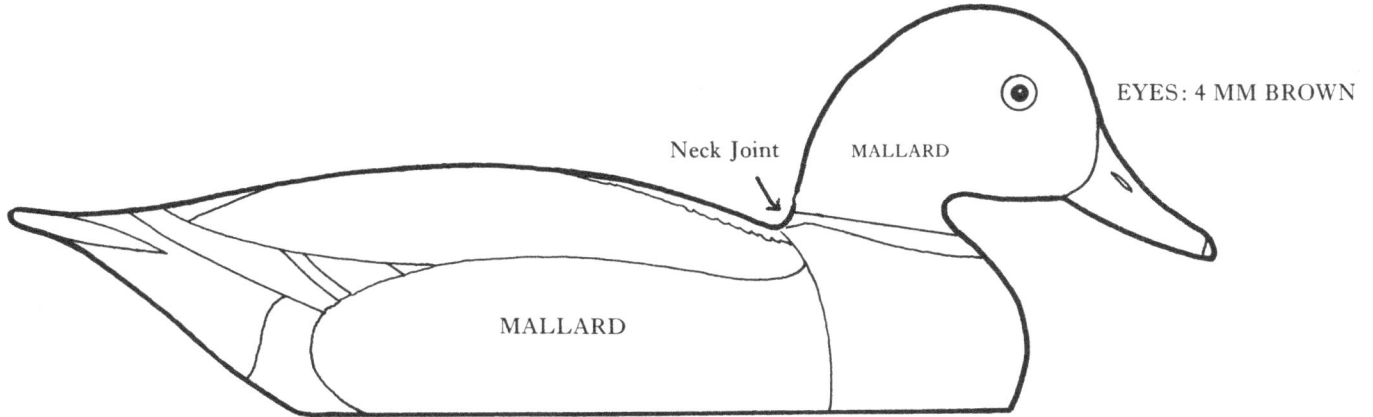

Neck Joint

MALLARD

EYES: 4 MM BROWN

MALLARD

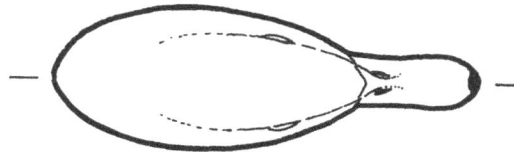

HEAD: TOP VIEW

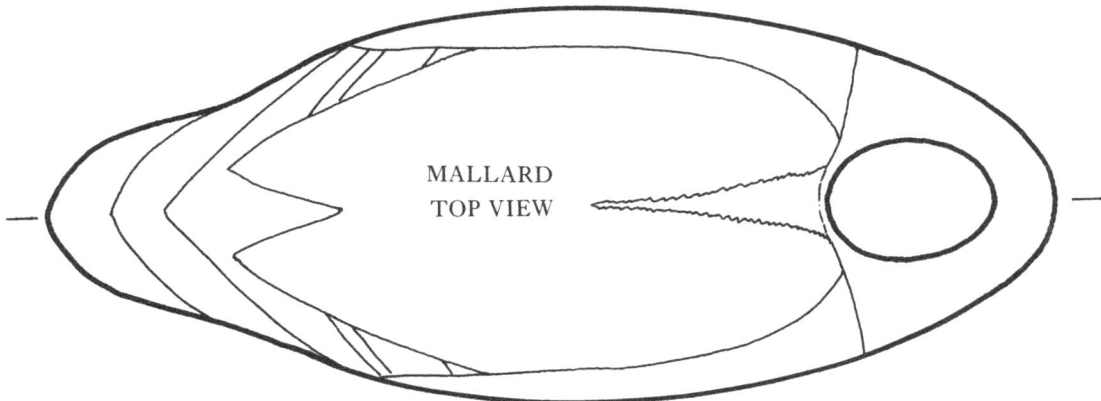

MALLARD
TOP VIEW

Plate 1.

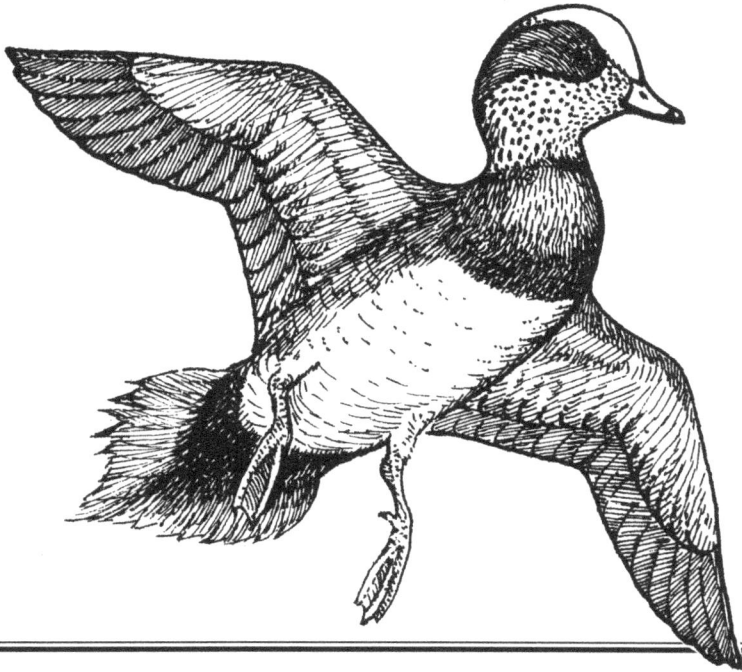

American Wigeon

Dimensions:
Head: 1⅝″ long × 1¼″ high × ⅝″ wide
Body: 4⅝″ long × 1³⁄₁₆″ high × 1⅞″ wide

EYES: 3 MM BROWN OR BLACK

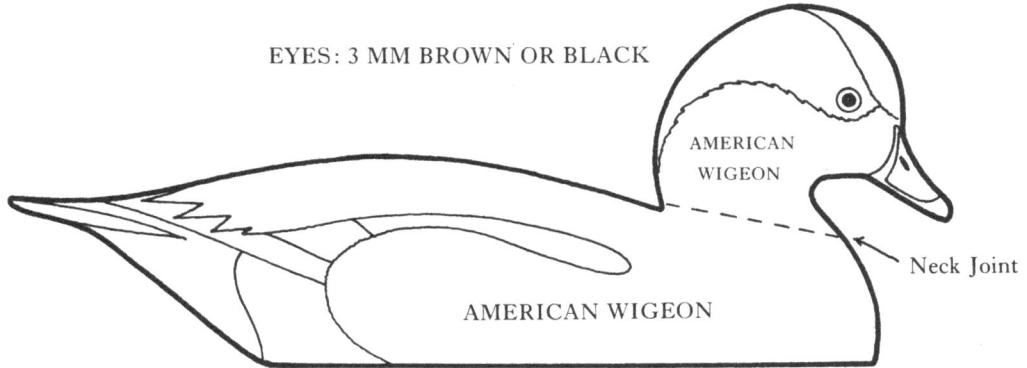

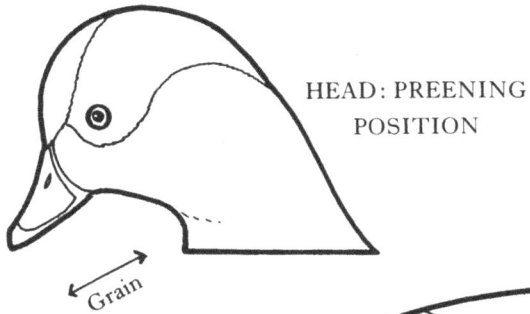

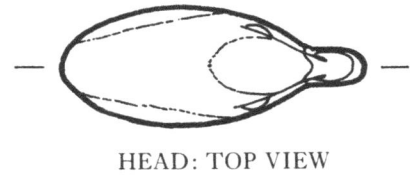

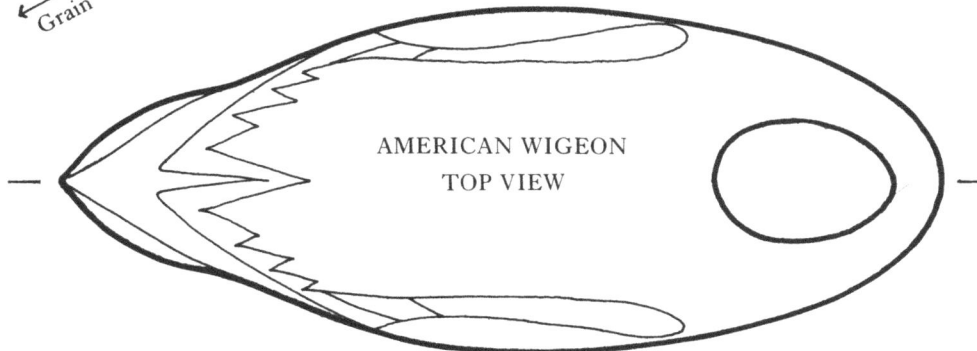

AMERICAN
WIGEON

Neck Joint

AMERICAN WIGEON

HEAD: PREENING
POSITION

Grain

HEAD: TOP VIEW

AMERICAN WIGEON
TOP VIEW

Plate 2.

Green-winged Teal

Dimensions:
Head: 1⅜" long × 1" high × ½" wide
Body: 3¹¹⁄₁₆" long × ⅞" high × 1½" wide

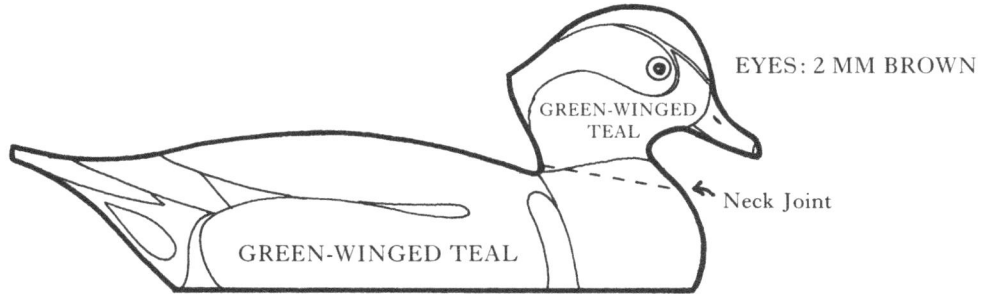

EYES: 2 MM BROWN

GREEN-WINGED TEAL

← Neck Joint

GREEN-WINGED TEAL

HEAD: FEMALE

HEAD (MALE): TOP VIEW

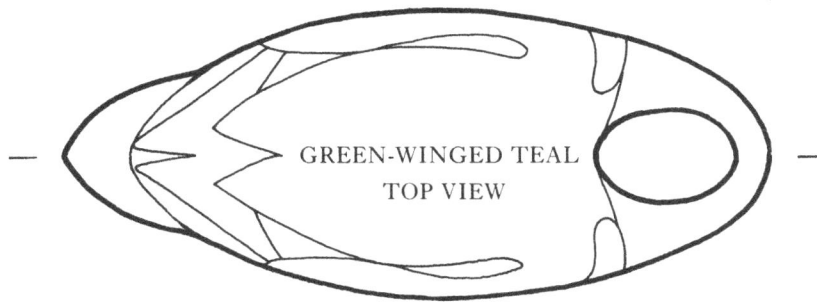

GREEN-WINGED TEAL
TOP VIEW

Plate 3.

TAKING OFF

Blue-winged Teal

Dimensions:
Head: 1⅝″ long × ¹⁵⁄₁₆″ high × 1¹⁄₁₆″ wide
Body: 4³⁄₁₆″ long × ¹⁵⁄₁₆″ high × 1¹¹⁄₁₆″ wide

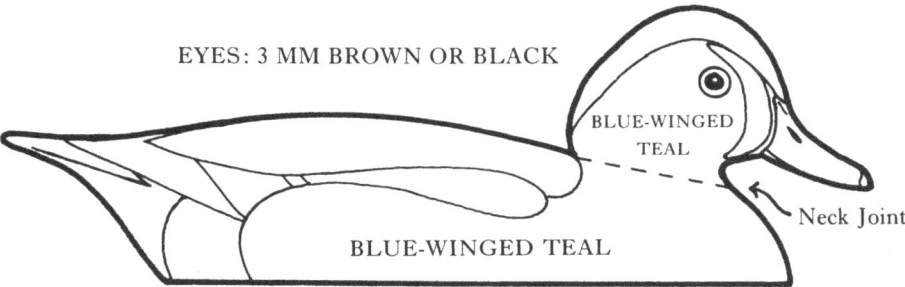

EYES: 3 MM BROWN OR BLACK

BLUE-WINGED TEAL

Neck Joint

BLUE-WINGED TEAL

HEAD: PREENING POSITION

HEAD: TOP VIEW

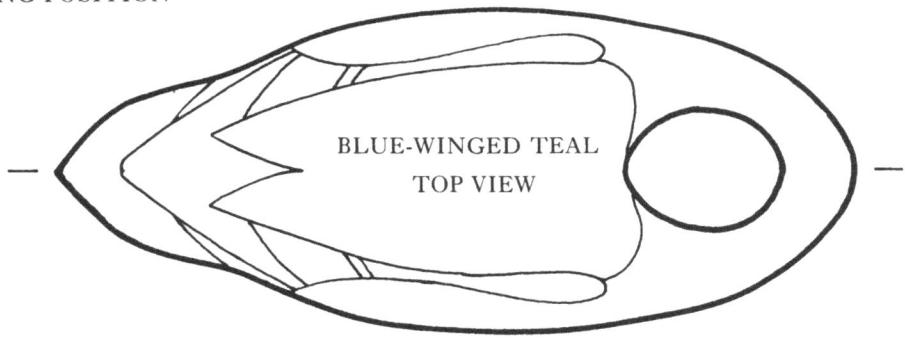

BLUE-WINGED TEAL
TOP VIEW

Plate 4.

Northern Shoveler

Dimensions:
Head: 2⅛″ long × 1³⁄₁₆″ high × ¹¹⁄₁₆″ wide
Body: 4⁷⁄₁₆″ long × 1³⁄₁₆″ high × 1¹⁵⁄₁₆″ wide

FEEDING

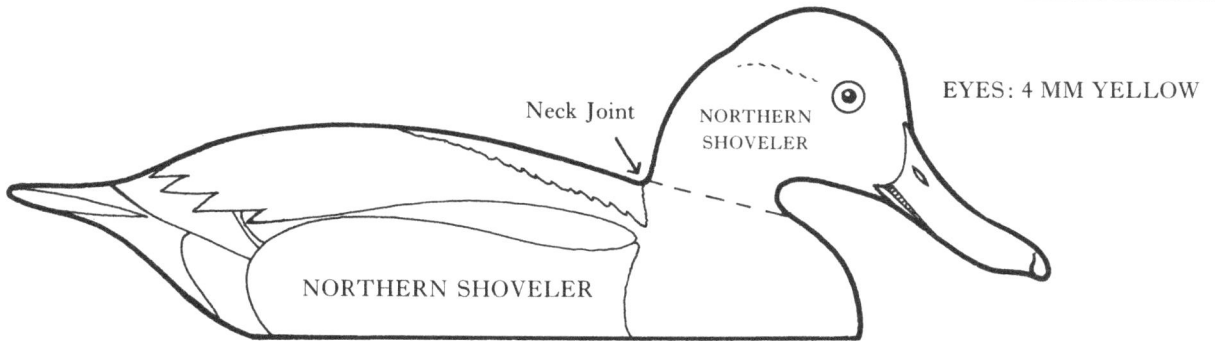

Neck Joint

NORTHERN SHOVELER

EYES: 4 MM YELLOW

NORTHERN SHOVELER

HEAD: LOW POSITION

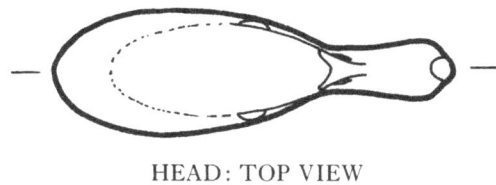

HEAD: TOP VIEW

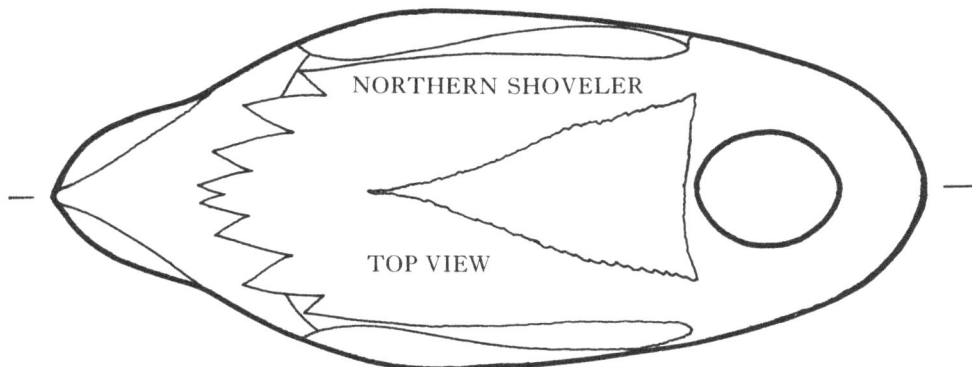

NORTHERN SHOVELER

TOP VIEW

Plate 5.

Common Pintail (Male)

Dimensions:
Head: $1\frac{15}{16}''$ long $\times$ $1\frac{3}{8}''$ high $\times$ $\frac{3}{4}''$ wide
Body: $6\frac{1}{2}''$ long $\times$ $1\frac{1}{4}''$ high $\times$ $2''$ wide

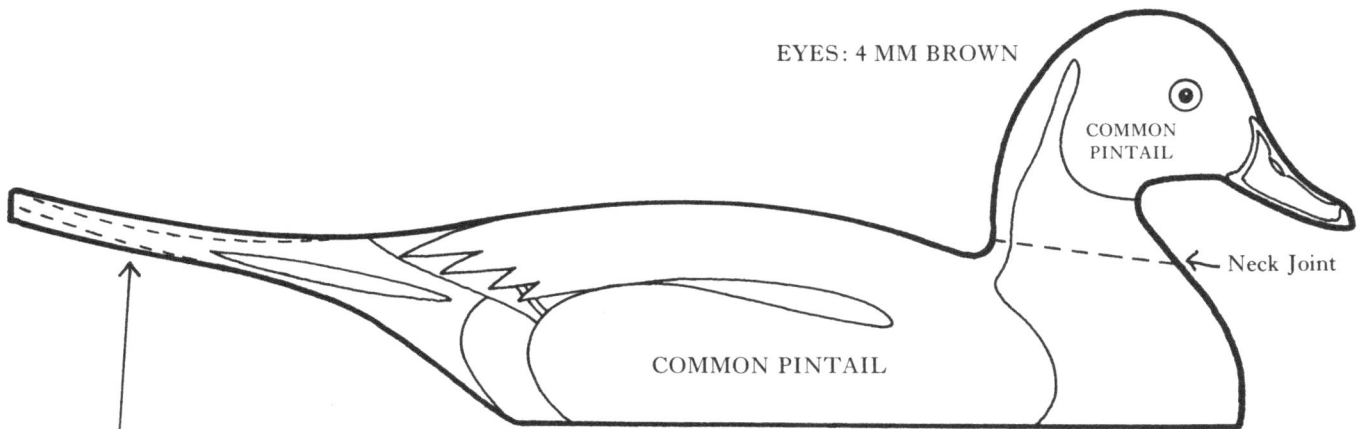

EYES: 4 MM BROWN

COMMON PINTAIL

Neck Joint

COMMON PINTAIL

Cut to dotted lines as final step in carving.

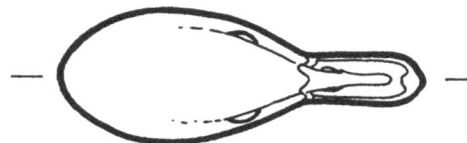

HEAD: TOP VIEW

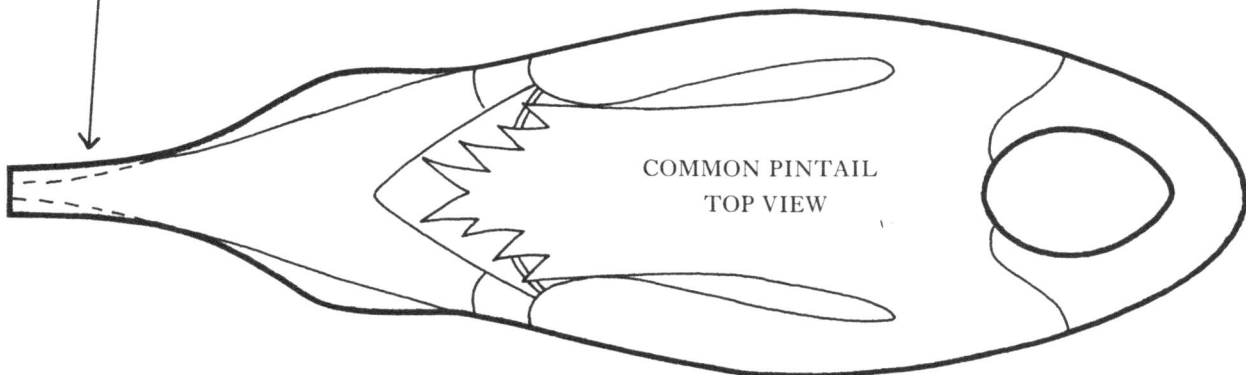

COMMON PINTAIL TOP VIEW

Plate 6.

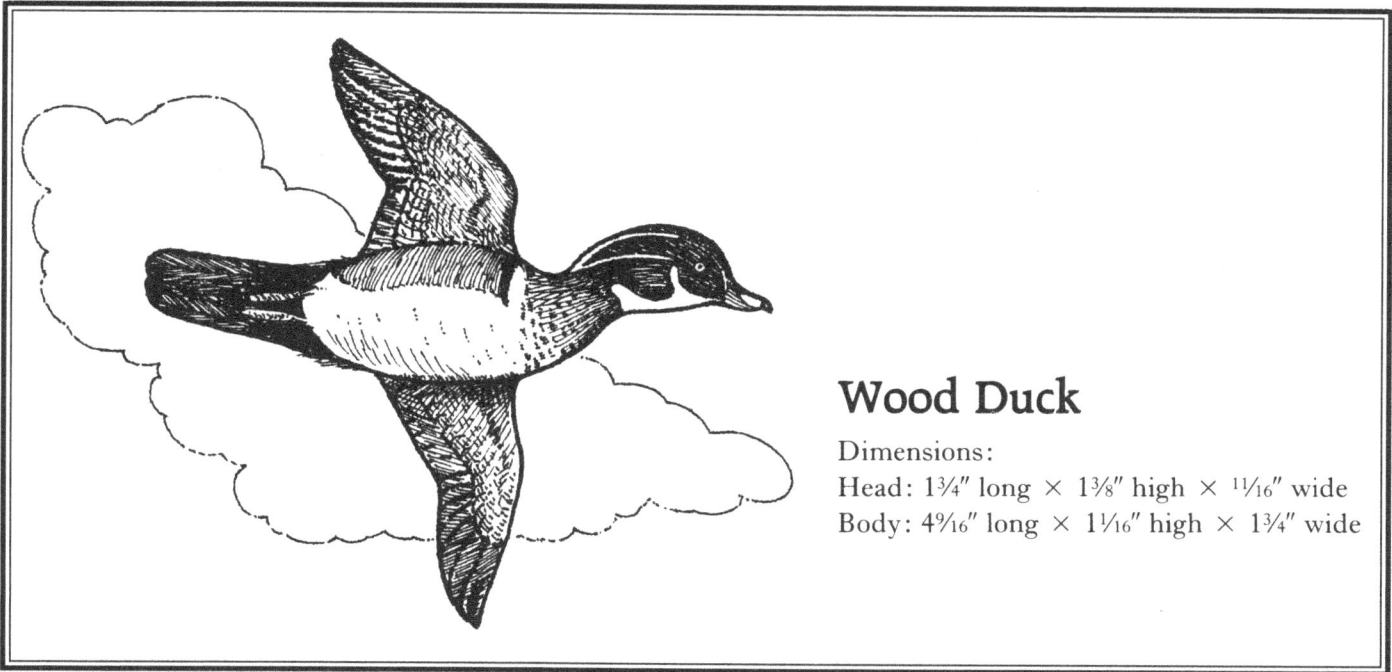

Wood Duck

Dimensions:
Head: 1¾″ long × 1⅜″ high × ¹¹⁄₁₆″ wide
Body: 4⁹⁄₁₆″ long × 1¹⁄₁₆″ high × 1¾″ wide

EYES: 4 MM RED, MALE
3 MM BROWN, FEMALE

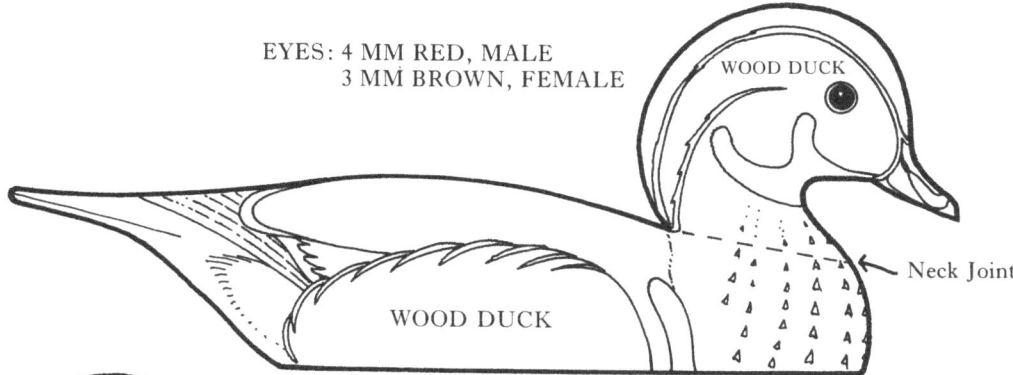

WOOD DUCK

WOOD DUCK

Neck Joint

HEAD: FEMALE

HEAD (MALE): TOP VIEW

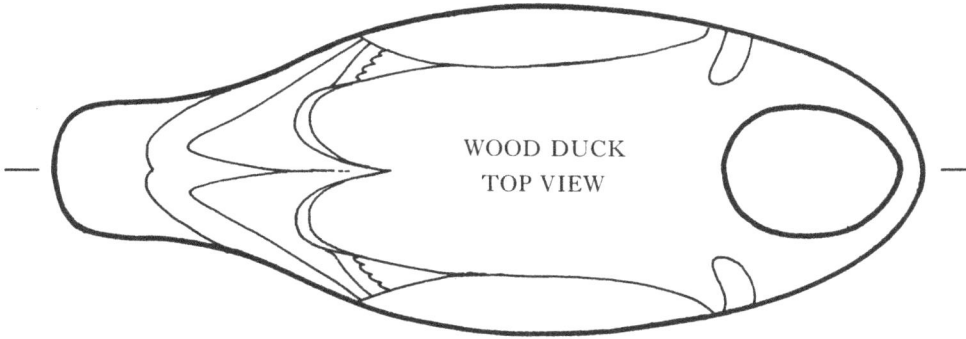

WOOD DUCK
TOP VIEW

Plate 7.

Canvasback

Dimensions:
Head: 2¹⁄₁₆″ long × 1⁵⁄₁₆″ high × ¾″ wide
Body: 4¹⁵⁄₁₆″ long × 1⅛″ high × 2³⁄₁₆″ wide

A CANVASBACK DECOY

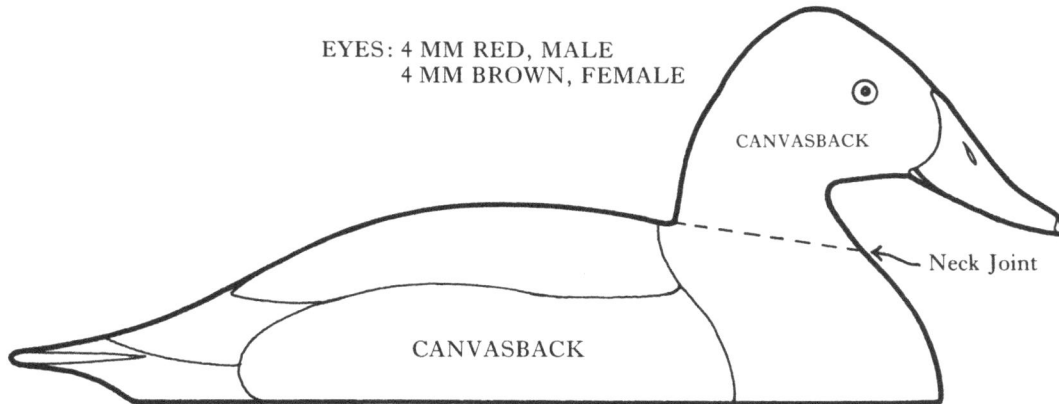

EYES: 4 MM RED, MALE
4 MM BROWN, FEMALE

CANVASBACK

Neck Joint

CANVASBACK

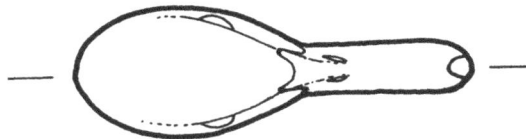

HEAD: TOP VIEW

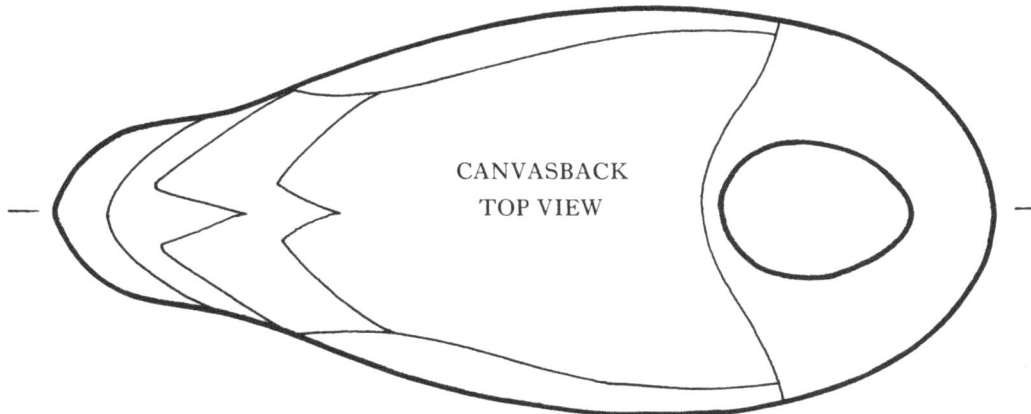

CANVASBACK
TOP VIEW

Plate 8.

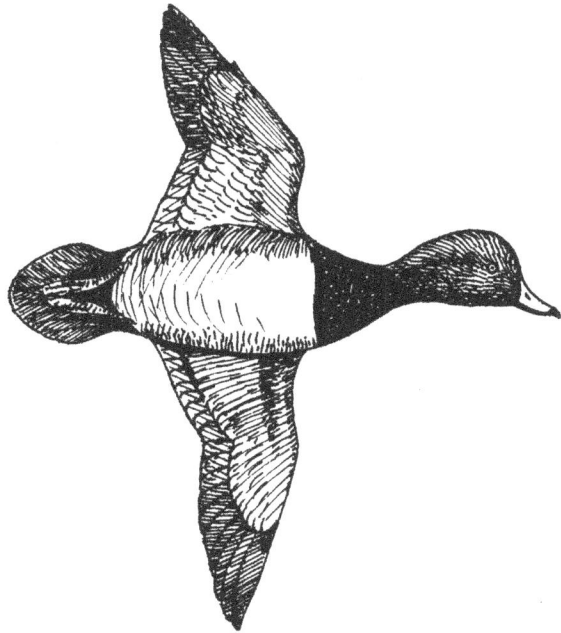

Redhead (or Scaup)

Dimensions:
Head: 1¾" long × 1⅜" high × ¾" wide
Body: 4⅜" long × 1" high × 2⅛" wide

EYES: 3 MM YELLOW, MALES
3 MM BROWN, FEMALES

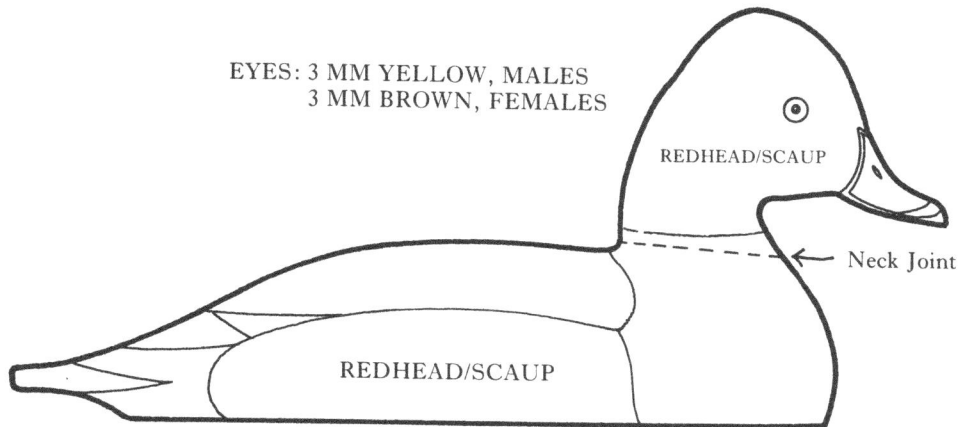

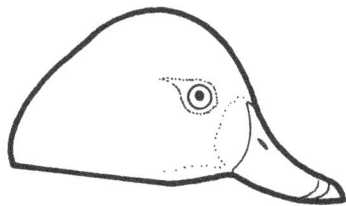

REDHEAD/SCAUP

Neck Joint

REDHEAD/SCAUP

HEAD (REDHEAD): FEMALE

HEAD (MALE): TOP VIEW

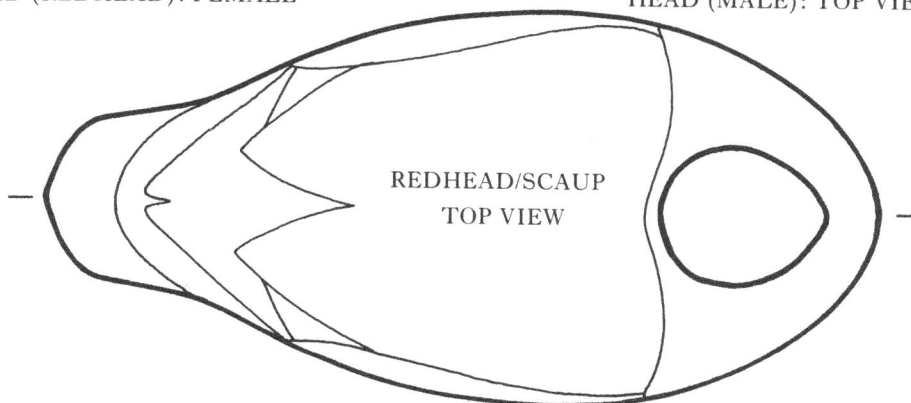

REDHEAD/SCAUP
TOP VIEW

Plate 9.

Ruddy Duck

Dimensions:
Head: $1\frac{11}{16}''$ long $\times$ $1\frac{1}{8}''$ high $\times$ $\frac{11}{16}''$ wide
Body: $3\frac{13}{16}''$ long $\times$ $\frac{3}{4}''$ high $\times$ $1\frac{13}{16}''$ wide

TAKING OFF

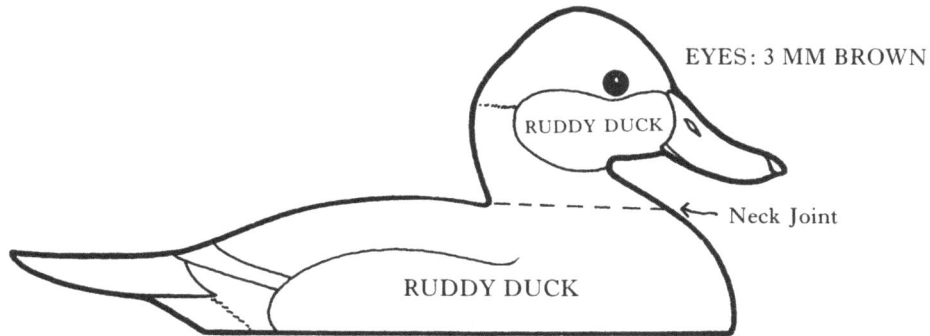

EYES: 3 MM BROWN

RUDDY DUCK

Neck Joint

RUDDY DUCK

HEAD: FEMALE

HEAD (MALE): TOP VIEW

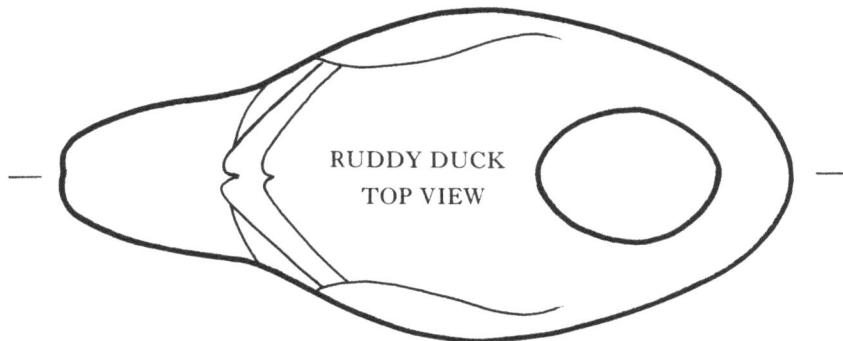

RUDDY DUCK
TOP VIEW

Plate 10.

Bufflehead

Dimensions:
Head: 1½" long × 1" high × ⅝" wide
Body: 3¹³⁄₁₆" long × ¹⁵⁄₁₆" high × 1⅝" wide

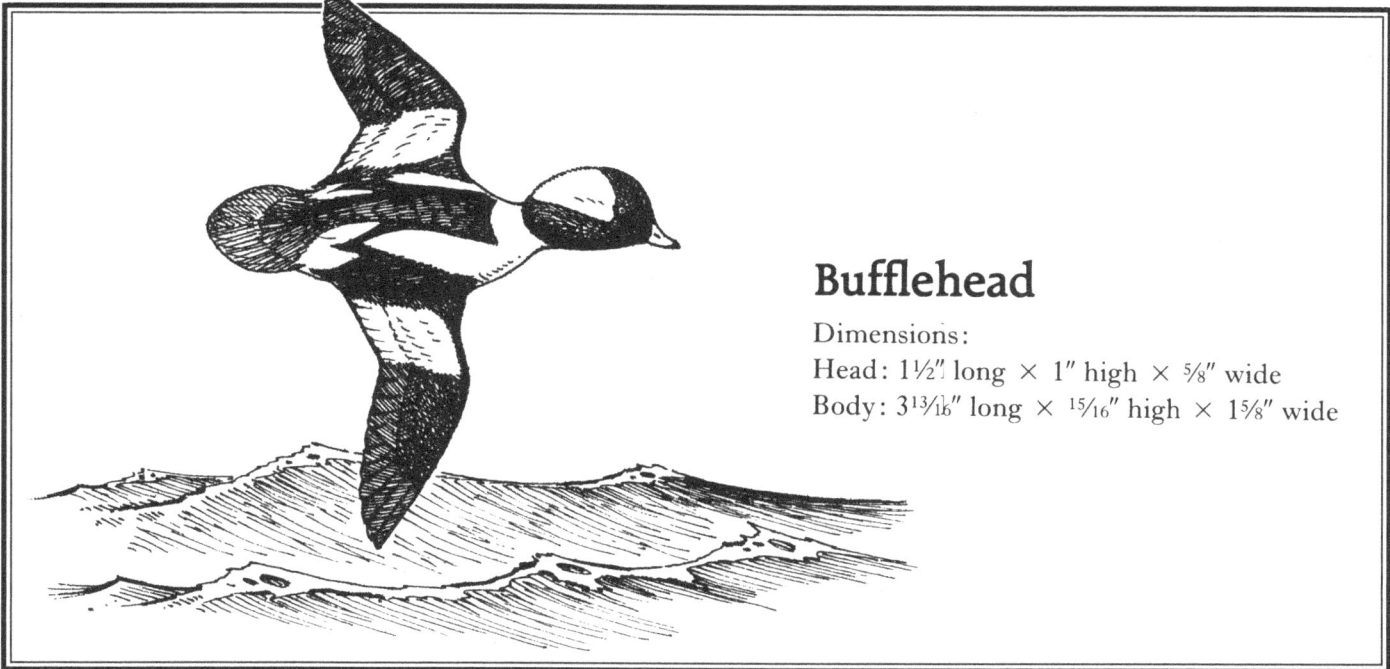

EYES: 4 MM BROWN OR BLACK

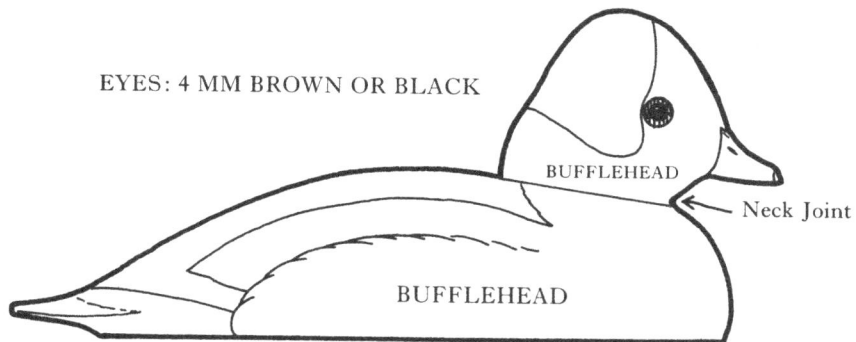

BUFFLEHEAD

Neck Joint

BUFFLEHEAD

HEAD: FEMALE

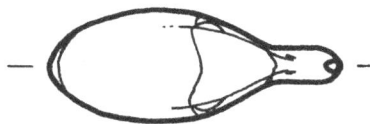

HEAD (MALE): TOP VIEW

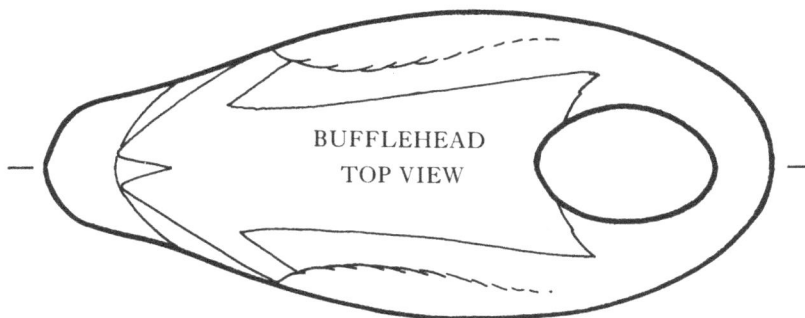

BUFFLEHEAD
TOP VIEW

Plate 11.

Common Eider

Dimensions:
Head: 2⁷⁄₁₆″ long × 1⁹⁄₁₆″ high × 1″ wide
Body: 6³⁄₁₆″ long × 1⁷⁄₁₆″ high × 3″ wide

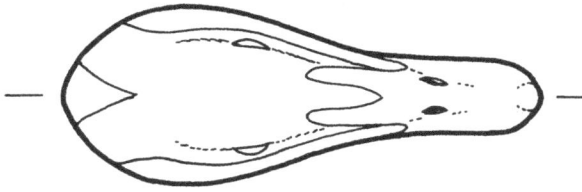

HEAD: TOP VIEW

EYES: 4 MM BROWN

COMMON EIDER

← Neck Joint

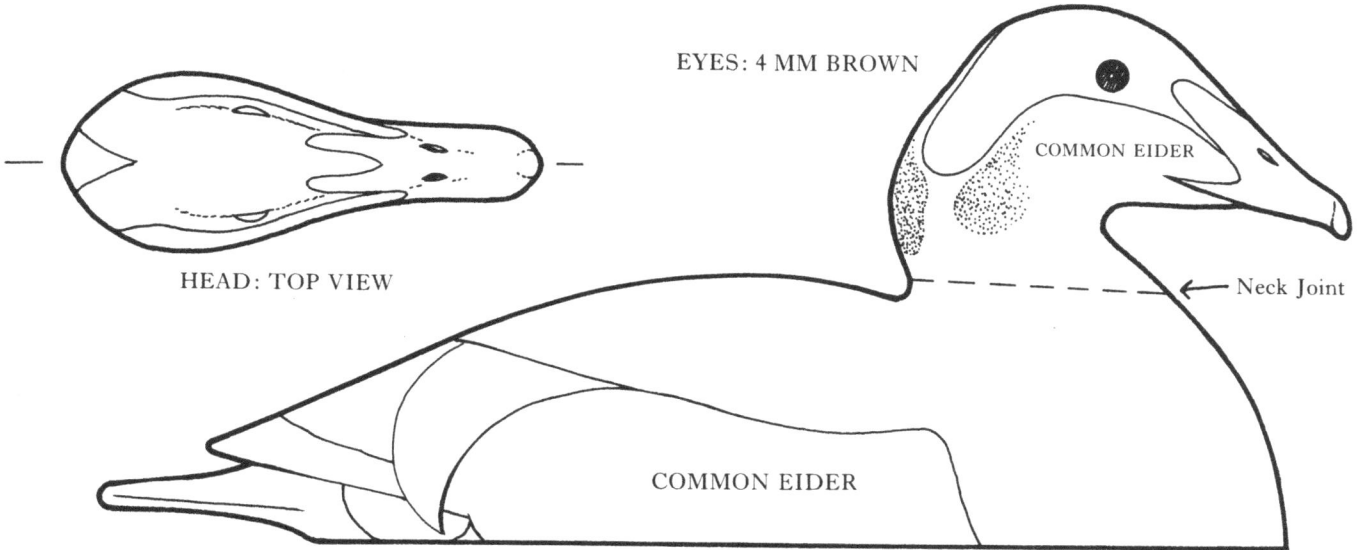

COMMON EIDER

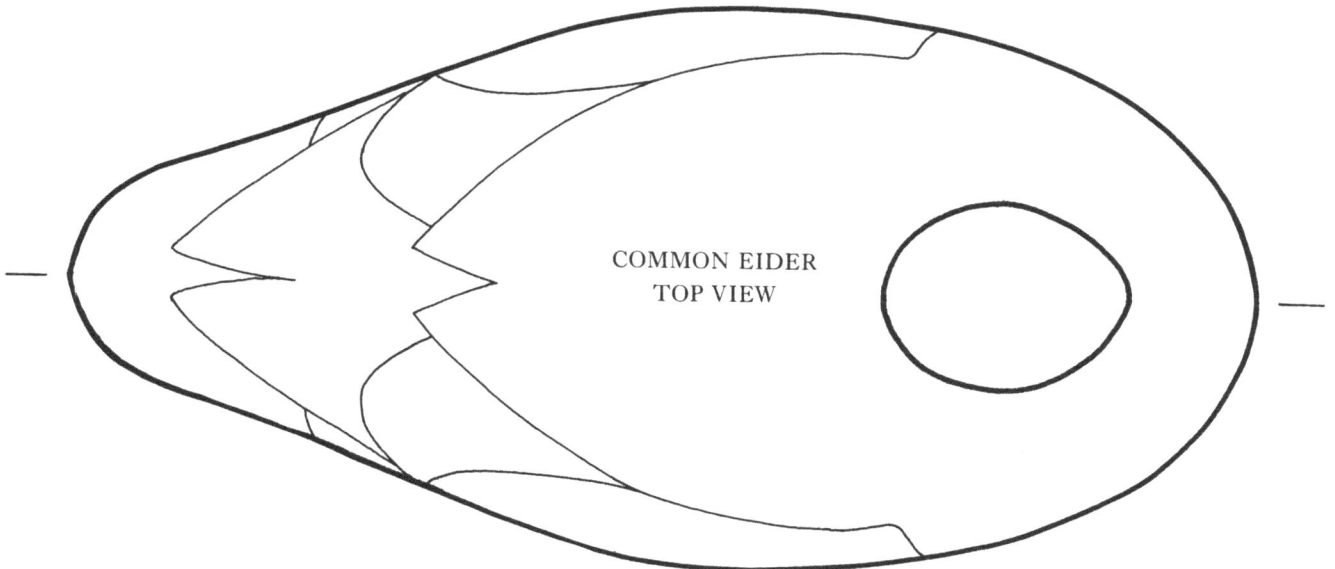

COMMON EIDER
TOP VIEW

Plate 12.

Hooded Merganser

Dimensions:
Head: $1\tfrac{15}{16}''$ long $\times$ $1\tfrac{3}{8}''$ high $\times$ $1\tfrac{1}{16}''$ wide
Body: $3\tfrac{15}{16}''$ long $\times$ $1\tfrac{3}{16}''$ high $\times$ $1\tfrac{9}{16}''$ wide

EYES: 4 MM YELLOW, MALE
4 MM BROWN, FEMALE

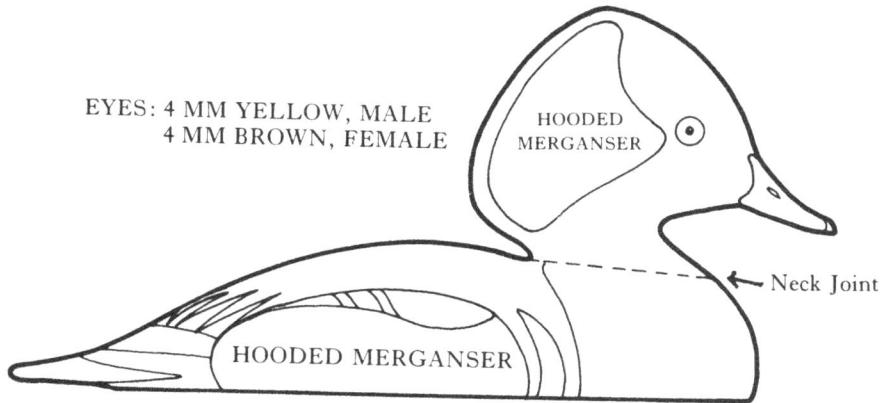

HOODED
MERGANSER

$\leftarrow$ Neck Joint

HOODED MERGANSER

HEAD: FEMALE

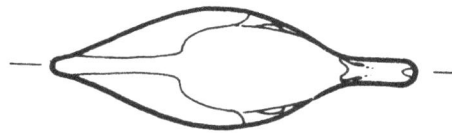

HEAD (MALE): TOP VIEW

HOODED
MERGANSER
TOP VIEW

Plate 13.

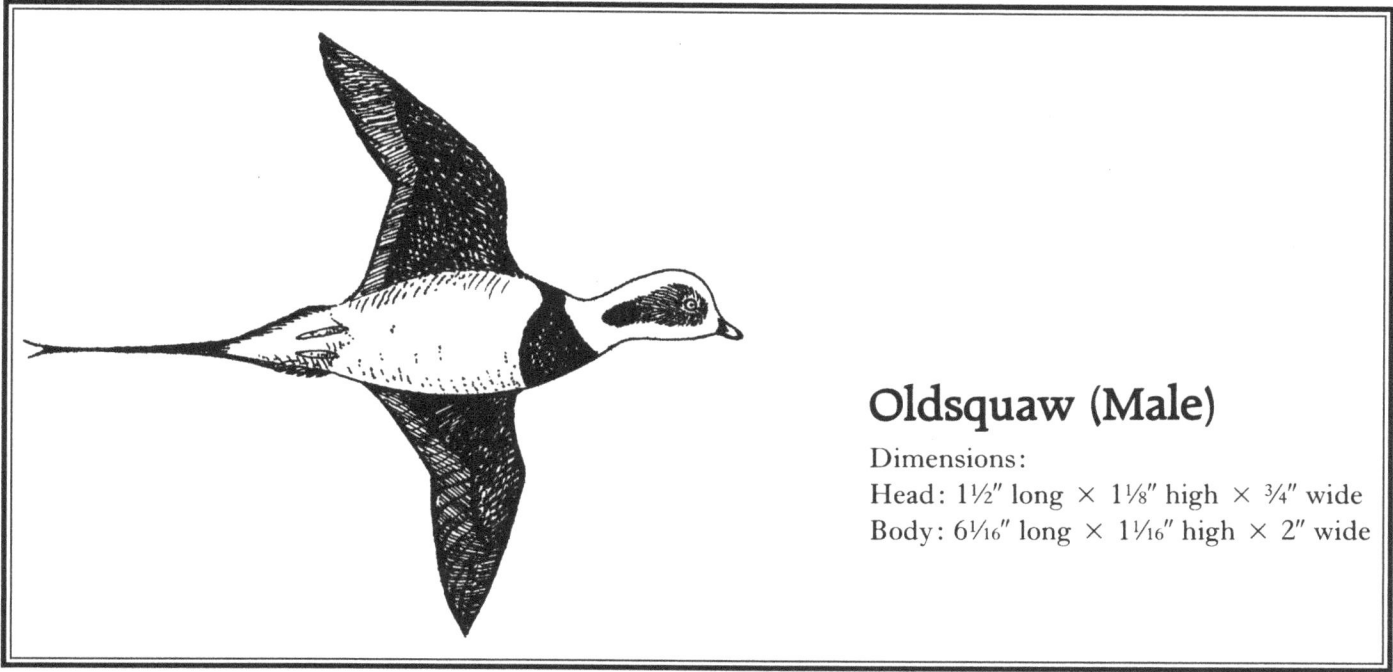

Oldsquaw (Male)

Dimensions:
Head: 1½" long × 1⅛" high × ¾" wide
Body: 6¹⁄₁₆" long × 1¹⁄₁₆" high × 2" wide

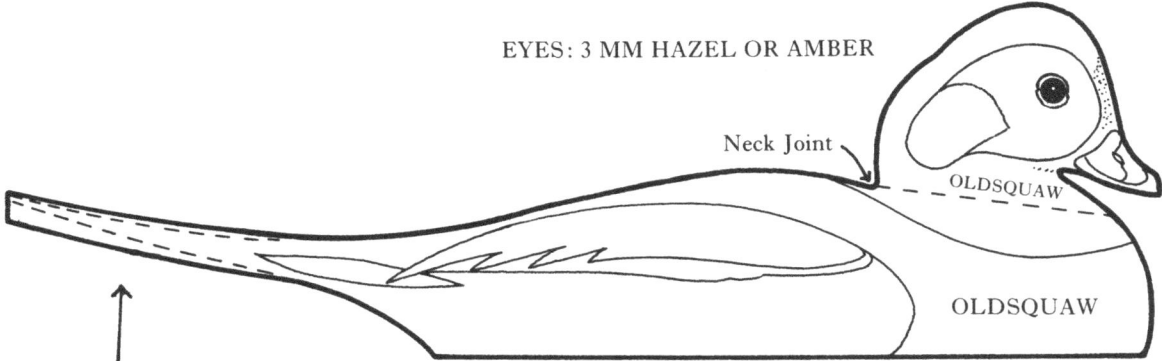

EYES: 3 MM HAZEL OR AMBER

Neck Joint

OLDSQUAW

OLDSQUAW

Cut to dotted lines as final step in carving.

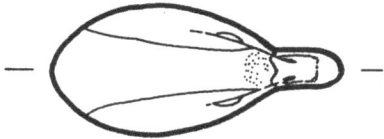

HEAD: TOP VIEW

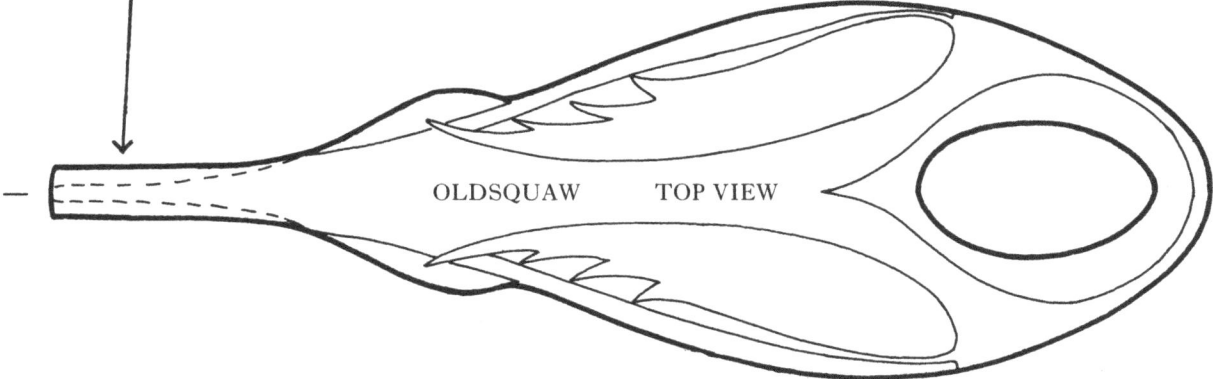

OLDSQUAW   TOP VIEW

Plate 14.

LANDING

Common Goldeneye

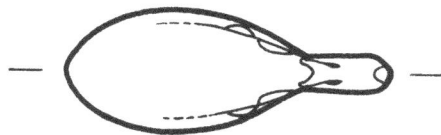

Dimensions:
Head: 1¾″ long × 1⁷⁄₁₆″ high × ¹¹⁄₁₆″ wide
Body: 4½″ long × 1″ high × 1¹⁵⁄₁₆″ wide

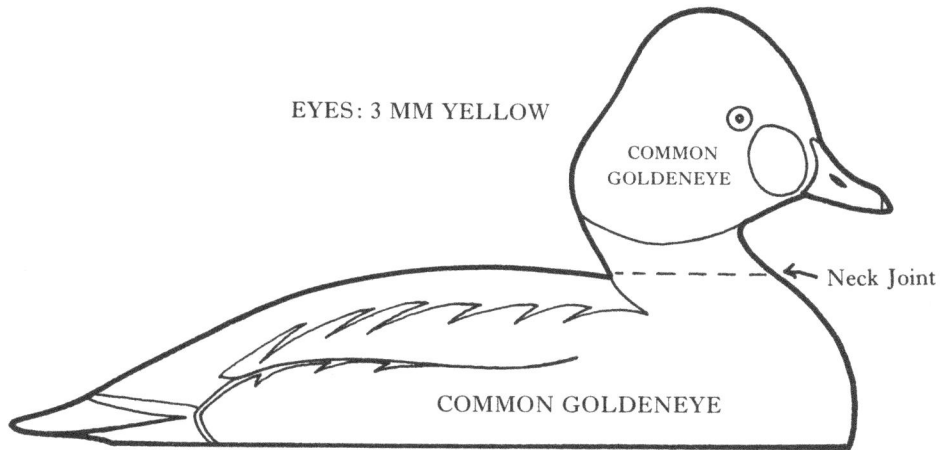

EYES: 3 MM YELLOW

COMMON
GOLDENEYE

Neck Joint

COMMON GOLDENEYE

HEAD: TOP VIEW

COMMON GOLDENEYE
TOP VIEW

Plate 15.

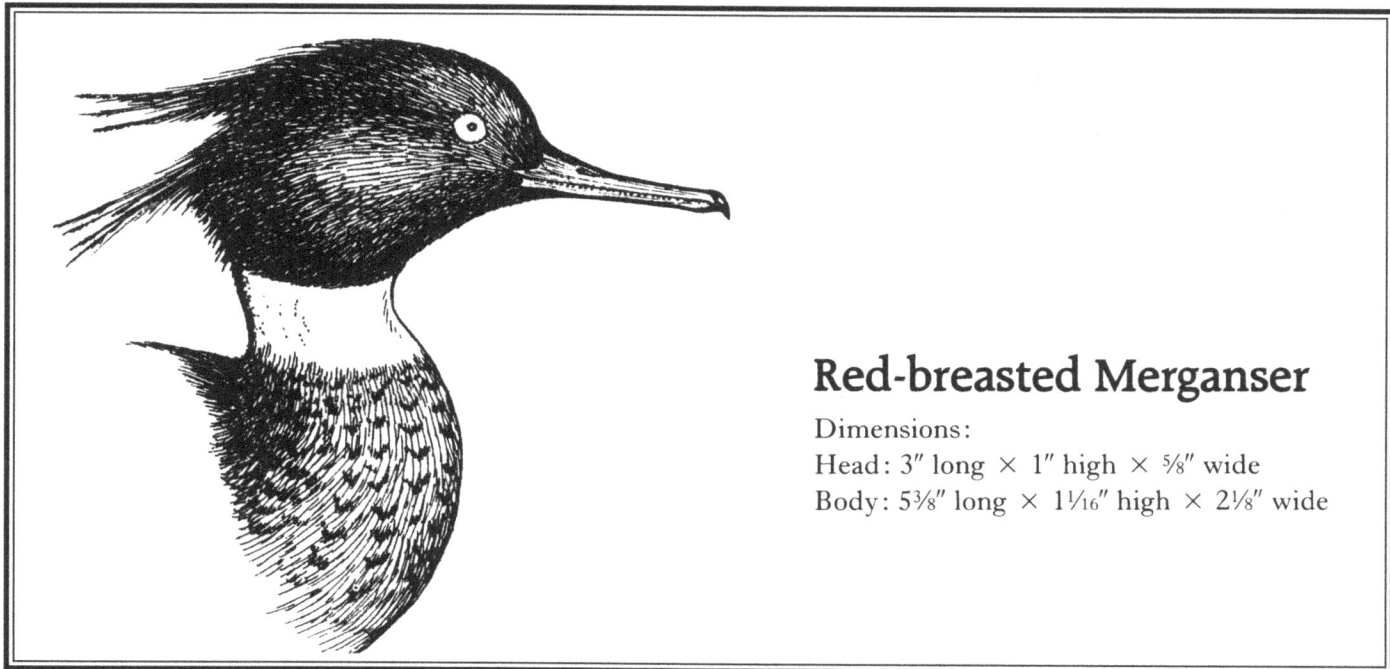

Red-breasted Merganser

Dimensions:
Head: 3″ long × 1″ high × ⅝″ wide
Body: 5⅜″ long × 1¹⁄₁₆″ high × 2⅛″ wide

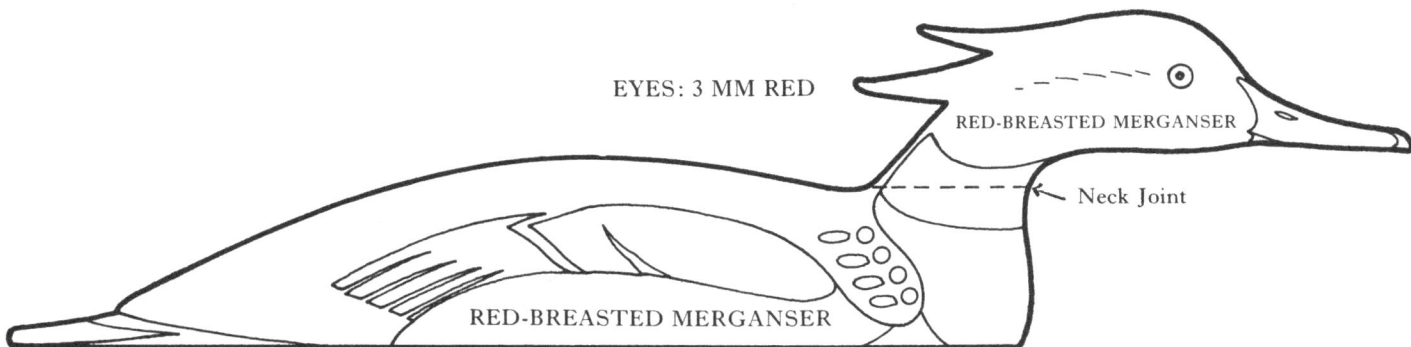

EYES: 3 MM RED

RED-BREASTED MERGANSER

Neck Joint

RED-BREASTED MERGANSER

HEAD: TOP VIEW

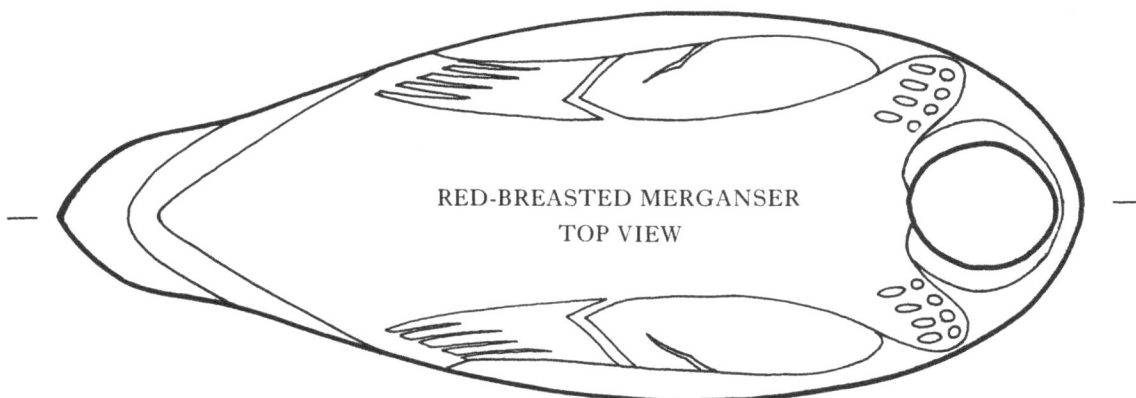

RED-BREASTED MERGANSER
TOP VIEW

Plate 16.

About the Author

Born in Atlantic City, New Jersey in 1948, the shore was rich in wildlife which held his youthful interest. Hunting was a prime activity since he was 14 years of age, and many full days were spent on marsh, field, and in the "Jersey pines." Tony was active as a commercial illustrator during the 1960s and developed a talent for drawing and painting local wildlife during this time. After service in the Marine Corps from 1968-70, he returned to painting wildlife and story illustration.

During the early 1970s he started to design and carve duck decoys for his own use. Soon he had requests from friends to make some birds for their gunning rigs. Woodcarving ultimately began to occupy more of his time and interest. While his carving origins started with decoys, somewhat more decorative birds, fish, and animals were requested by many patrons of his art. Most of his work is done in white cedar; he also carved in basswood, butternut, mahogany, maple, ebony, oak, and several species of pine. The painted finish of his bird and fish carvings are what help to make each carving special.

Mr. Hillman has authored and illustrated over 30 carving and painting how-to books, most with Dover Publications. Three of the earliest titles were done with Harry V. Shourds, the grandson of the famous Tuckerton carver. Thousands of wood carvers have used their series of carving and painting patterns for over thirty years. Tony added other titles which included several painting how-to books, fish carving, and weathervane subjects. Tony was invited to Washington, D.C. to the American Folk Life Festival in 1983 by the Smithsonian Institute to demonstrate his craft, one of only 3 carvers in the state to be so honored.

He still carves full-time and his favorite subjects are the shorebirds which migrate to and from our coast each year. Tony has lived in Cape May County for the past thirty years, and his carvings reflect a lifetime of careful observation of our unique coastal heritage. Since 1999 his presence on the internet has allowed Hillman to spend more time carving and selling directly to patrons, rather than attending scattered shows around the country. His website, www.HillmanArt.com, features several from a selection of hundreds of original works, with directions to his home and contact information.

www.ingramcontent.com/pod-product-compliance
Lightning Source LLC
Chambersburg PA
CBHW060902090426
42738CB00025B/3498